THEN & NOW

WASHINGTON COUNTY

I0809482

Opposite: Two women and a young boy pose for a photograph in a millinery shop in Copan, Oklahoma, in its early days. Many small towns in Oklahoma had specialized shops to serve the needs of their growing communities. (Historical photograph courtesy Bartlesville Area History Museum.)

THEN & NOW

WASHINGTON COUNTY

Michelle M. Martin

To my fellow "history rock stars,"
Jo Crabtree, Julie Daniels, Kay Little, and Debbie Neece!
Long may you continue to explore the wonders of history
and share them with others!
In fond memory of my mentor and friend Dr. Peter Schmitt,
for whom the best history was local history.
Thank you for your guidance, wisdom, and friendship.

Copyright © 2010 by Michelle M. Martin
ISBN 978-0-7385-7744-9

Library of Congress Control Number: 2009939981

Published by Arcadia Publishing
Charleston SC, Chicago IL, Portsmouth NH, San Francisco CA

Printed in the United States of America

For all general information contact Arcadia Publishing at:
Telephone 843-853-2070
Fax 843-853-0044
E-mail sales@arcadiapublishing.com
For customer service and orders:
Toll-Free 1-888-313-2665

Visit us on the Internet at www.arcadiapublishing.com

On the Front Cover: Pictured standing next to the pump jack of the Nellie V. Johnstone No. 1 oil well in Bartlesville, Oklahoma, George Keeler was one of the founding fathers of Bartlesville. His business ventures included storekeeping and the emerging oil industry. Today a historically accurate replica of the fully operational Nellie V. Johnstone No. 1 is a part of Discovery 1 Park. A community education effort, Discovery 1 Park pays homage to the first commercial oil well in Oklahoma history and seeks to preserve that crucial history and share it with future generations. An officially recognized Oklahoma centennial project in 2007, eventual plans for the park include outdoor exhibits and a visitor center. (Historic photograph courtesy Bartlesville Area History Museum; modern photograph courtesy the author.)

On the Back Cover: Citizens gather on Ochelata's Main Street near the bank for a photograph. (Historic photograph courtesy Bartlesville Area History Museum.)

Contents

Foreword

After a 30-year journalism career at CBS and several years at the helm of my own production company, I returned to my home state of Kansas and rediscovered small town America. While driving my parents in the countryside west of Independence, Kansas, (my hometown) I was in awe of the beauty and majesty of the Kansas landscape. When I fell in love with the tall-grass prairie and bought my ranch, I felt a sense of responsibility toward the small town of Sedan, Kansas. It was vanishing before my very eyes, a small town that seemed destined to disappear—and with it our core American values and way of life. Never one to shrink from a challenge, I embarked upon a one-man historical preservation mission. Buying buildings and restoring them gave me a good feeling; a sense that I had preserved something for future generations.

When I purchased a radio station in Bartlesville, Oklahoma, I also found myself adding another historical property to my collection—the Pioneer Building. Constructed in 1910 and home to the Pioneer Telephone Company, I fell in love not just with the building, but also with the potential that restoring it to its former glory held for downtown Bartlesville. For me, saving a piece of downtown history was just as important as filling the building with tenants. In 2010, the Pioneer Building will celebrate its centennial, and I hope that 100 years from now the blue bells on its stone facade will be as bright and charming as they are today. Preserving our rich American historical narrative is up to all of us so future generations will know how far we have progressed as a nation and will appreciate our past.

—Bill Kurtis

Acknowledgments

For an author, the most difficult part of any work is acknowledging all the individuals and organizations that help make a work such as this possible. I feel that much credit is due to my family and close friends: my parents, Dale and Susan Martin; my brother, Michael; his wife, Amelia; my nephew, Nicholas; my dear friends from my days in Fort Scott, Kansas: Arnold Schofield, Rosemary Frey, Alan Chilton, Carolyn Cooper, Alice Claypool, Deb Goodrich, and Kari West; my new friends in Bartlesville, Dewey, and Ramona: Kay and Harvey Little, Jo and Gene Crabtree, Sandy Haberly, Vickie Gates, Scott Perkins, Linda Stone, Duane Price, and Julie and Charlie Daniels. Thank you all for your support and advice. I wish to thank the staff of the Bartlesville Area History Museum for their contributions to this work. Without the extensive Frank Griggs photograph collection, this work would not have been possible. Special thanks to photograph archivist Debbie Neece for her attention to detail and dedication to helping make this project a reality. Debbie is by far the most efficient photograph archivist with whom I have ever worked. Individuals like Debbie make this process enjoyable and easier for an author. Thanks is also due to Jo Crabtree for her advice and input, including the inclusion of her historical home in Ramona, Oklahoma, in this work. Her husband, Gene, was a valuable resource in identifying locations in Ramona. Kay Little also deserves much praise for her guidance and assistance as well. Kay took to the roads and walked the streets of our towns with me, looking for the past. Her enthusiasm was contagious and kept me going! Thanks also to Joan Singleton, director of the Bartlesville Area History Museum, for the generosity of the museum in sharing its photograph collections. Unless otherwise noted, all historical photographs are courtesy of Bartlesville Area History Museum. All modern photographs are the work of the author.

My last acknowledgment of thanks must go to my late mentor and friend, Dr. Peter Schmitt of Western Michigan University. Dr. Schmitt was responsible for guiding my undergraduate studies in American material culture and local history. He always demanded the best from me as a student and implored me to excel above and beyond all expectations set for me. His love of local history has guided my work as I have moved from Michigan to Kansas and now to Oklahoma. I can never repay him for the guidance and friendship he bestowed upon me—I can only continue in his footsteps and share history with future generations.

Introduction

Nestled in the northeast portion of Oklahoma, Washington County boasts a unique geography and history. Bordering Kansas to the north, Washington County was formed from lands inhabited by the Cherokee, Delaware, and Osage tribes. The first white settlements in the county are credited to Nelson Carr and Jacob Bartles, both former members of the 6th Kansas Cavalry, who arrived here after the close of the American Civil War. They were just the first of many homesteaders that would flood into the territory after the war. Through the medium of historical and modern photographs, this volume will examine a period of American history that is romanticized, yet not often fully understood. The age of the wildcatter and oilman was born in Washington County, and fortunes were made and lost many times over. Luck rode the winds as the age of the American Indian, roaming the prairies in unbridled freedom, came to an end in the name of progress. The Indian Territory that would become Oklahoma was the destination of those seeking freedom, progress, and prosperity. They would all come to call Washington County and its cities—Copan, Dewey, Bartlesville, Ramona, Vera, and Ochelata—home. Today this county is as vibrant and rich in its traditions as our pioneer forebearers.

In today's fast-paced world that never seems to slow down for a moment, it is easy for one to forget what has come before us. When I pull out of my driveway and head north on Delaware Avenue, most of the time I am concerned with how heavy the traffic on Adams Boulevard will be when I reach the intersection. While sitting in the research room of the Bartlesville Area History Museum looking at a black-and-white image on the screen, my entire perception of my morning drive changes in an instant. There it was before my eyes—the very street I drive every day, in its earliest incarnation. A dirt street with stables, houses, blacksmiths, corrals, and all kinds of buildings teeming with life was there for me to rediscover. From that moment on, my drive time on Delaware Avenue changed. Instead of hurrying along my way, I found myself paying more attention to my surroundings. I began to wonder who had lived on my street before me and what they had experienced while living in the fledgling city of Bartlesville, Indian Territory. This curiosity about the past spurred me to delve into the rich historical photographic collection left behind by Frank Griggs. A frontier photographer, Griggs arrived in Washington County in 1908, and for more than 60 years, he documented the life of the county and its residents. For me, this book is the blending of my two greatest passions—historical research and my love of photography. In a small way, I feel as if I am walking in the footsteps of Frank Griggs, and with every click of the shutter, I now preserve history much in the same way he did so many years ago.

CHAPTER 1

Hustle and Bustle

Street Scenes

This view of early day Ramona, Oklahoma, founded in 1899, shows the variety of homes and businesses that once thrived in the community. The oil, gas, and cattle industries fueled its growth, and like many Oklahoma towns, Ramona seemed to skyrocket almost overnight. Once the oil and gas dried up, the growth slowed, and today Ramona is a quiet agricultural town that hangs onto several reminders of its once bustling, glorious past.

This view of downtown Ramona looking northeast shows the diversity of buildings that once adorned its main street. On the corner is the Bryce Grocery. Residents could obtain dry goods, kitchen utensils, sundries, shoes, and hats—just to name a few of the items available there. With a mix of brick and wood-frame buildings, Ramona boasted a bustling population. Today a small apartment complex stands in place of the Bryce Grocery. Many buildings that once adorned the street are gone as well.

Another view of downtown Ramona, just two years after Oklahoma gained statehood in 1909, shows continued growth. With revenues from oil, gas, and the cattle trade flowing in, city businesses were profitable. The same view is altered today. The only recognizable structure left is the bank building. To save the historical structure, the top floor was removed and the lower level saved. The building entrance is much as it was in its heyday, and inside, the massive safe still remains.

North of Dewey, Oklahoma, Copan is now primarily an agricultural community. In its glory days, Copan boasted a thriving Main Street, with M. F. Nelson General Merchandise, the post office, a bank, and a shoe repair shop. With so many wood-frame buildings, Copan fell prey to a massive fire that ravaged its downtown. All of the buildings pictured here were lost. Some of the structures built after the fire remain.

Eighth Street (now Don Tyler Avenue) became the heart of the downtown Dewey business district after Dewey Street's development. This scene, looking west from Shawnee Street toward the Dewey Hotel (right) and the Bartles home and store (left), shows the community development. With interurban tracks in the center of the streets, the photograph was taken sometime between 1907 and 1909. The view is similar today. With many historical buildings still along the street, the city remains vibrant and full of life.

This view of downtown Dewey, taken in the late 1910s, looks west toward the Dewey Hotel. With sturdy brick buildings, a streetcar in the middle of the street, and people shopping and conducting business, Dewey's prosperity is evident. The light dusting of snow on the streets hints at the time of year. The view of Dewey and its streets is much the same today.

In the 1910s and 1920s, downtown Dewey boasted a thriving business district. This view of the south side of Eighth Street looking west shows the range of businesses in town. With Green Real Estate, the office of Dr. George Cox, and the Security National Bank (with tall spire), downtown thrived. The street scene is similar in modern times, and vestiges of the past can be seen in the surviving buildings. Antique stores, small shops, and independent businesses still make up the core of downtown Dewey.

Taken from the third-floor turret of the Dewey Hotel, this photograph from the early 20th century shows a community preparing for celebration. With red, white, and blue streamers, bunting, and a plethora of American flags, the view of Eighth Street (now Don Tyler Avenue) looking east is festive and inviting. The view is much the same today. Paved streets and taller trees are the most pronounced changes.

The Gem Theater (also known as the Yale) was a hub of activity in Dewey. Seen below promoting the Dewey bingo hall, the theater is flanked to the east by the J&M Lumber Company. Residents fondly recall Saturday matinees there. Later in its days as a theater, the Gem showed films of an adult nature, and locals recall the "Dewey Dirties." Today the former theater is home to Barking Dog Designs, and the former lumber company is occupied by Kay's Corner Antiques.

On October 15, 1917, a group gathered on Third Street between the *Daily Enterprise* newspaper and Parrett's store building to hear the results of the final World Series game, in which the Chicago White Sox defeated the New York Giants. The *Daily Enterprise*, located at 120 West Third Street, posted scores in the window. On the right are two Bartlesville Interurban Railway Company cars, which operated from Dewey through Bartlesville to Smeltertown, located just southwest of Bartlesville by National Zinc. Today Parrett's is home to the 2 Sisters Pub and Grille.

By the 1920s, Bartlesville's Third Street teemed with activity. With interurban tracks and angled automobile parking, Bartlesville was on the move. The north block (left) contained a garment shop, a shoe store, a café, a boardinghouse, Musselman Abstract Company, and Griggs Studio, one of Bartlesville's photography studios. The opposite block contained Star Dollar Store, Degen's, and Drum Studio, Bartlesville's other photography studio. The Washington County Courthouse (center) boasted the words "Washington County" atop its roof, and at night they illuminated the city street.

In a set of brick buildings on the north side of Second Street, between Dewey Avenue and Johnstone Street, several businesses were established to serve Bartlesville's growing population. Govreau's Harness, Saddles, and Buggies, and Berentz Hardware, Furniture, and Undertaking were located at 110–112 Second Street. Joseph Govreau opened his establishment in 1897, and in 1940, the business was still in the same location. William T. Berentz came from Indiana to Bartlesville. In 1901, he opened his hardware, furniture, and undertaking parlor.

With the boom of the oil industry, Bartlesville prospered and businesses catered to the needs of a new age. The photograph below, taken on Fourth Street looking west from Osage Avenue, shows the impact of the oil. With filling stations, tire service centers, and automobile garages on Fourth Street, Bartlesville was a true oil town. The REDA Pump Building, to the left, stands out as one of the tallest structures. To its right is the second city hall. The view now is somewhat similar.

Early in Bartlesville's history Second Street was the primary business district. Developing from Bartlesville's southern settlement on the south side of the Caney River, Second Street boasted many grand buildings. In 1898, George Keeler erected this two-story building (shown below). He named the building the Josie Keeler Building after his second wife. Many establishments have called the northwest corner of Johnstone and Second Streets home, including Wolcott's Grocery, Eureka Drug Store, and a furniture store. The structure was lost to a fire in 1963, and today it is a parking lot.

This is a view of Third Street looking west from atop the Washington County Courthouse. To the left one can see the unique domed roof of the city hall and fire station, and immediately to its right the three-story Pioneer Building stands out. The Congress and Almeda Hotels are the tallest structures seen to the right. An interurban car can be seen nearing the intersection of Third and Cherokee Streets. Many of the original buildings seen in this view are still here today.

This photograph of the north side of Second Street, between Dewey Avenue and Osage Street, in 1906 shows businesses in Bartlesville. The corner contained the Magnet Groceries and Meat Market, and the Modern Studio, where photographs were created. Next to Magnet Groceries was the F. W. Weeks Building, constructed in 1903. The Weeks Building was home to the Star Theatorium, the first motion picture theater in Bartlesville. Later the Buford Building (Congress Hotel) was built next to Magnet Groceries. Today all are in use.

CHAPTER 2

MAKING A BUCK

BUSINESSES

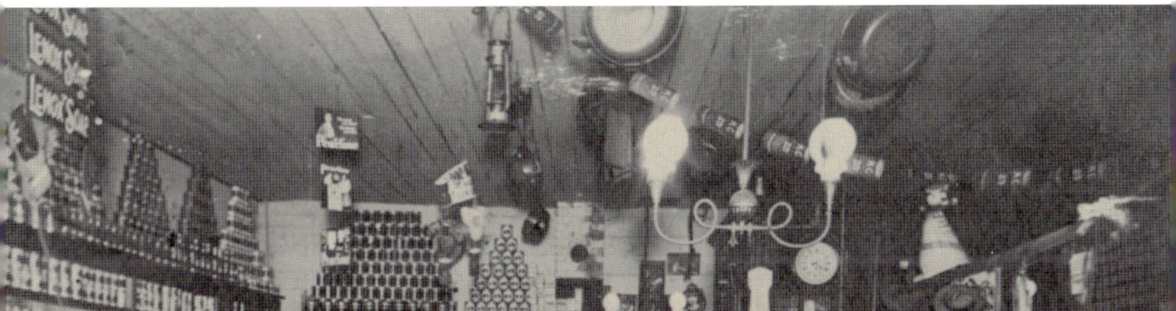

In Ramona, the Carnahan Grocery was one of the many locations to buy goods. Here a group of men gather in the store, surrounded by all manner of goods. With wooden floors and ceilings, the store is packed from the floor to the rafters with canned goods, lanterns, dishes, and other household items. Taken in 1916, this photograph also shows how life was changing in small towns with the introduction of gaslight. Seen hanging from the ceiling, the gaslight fixture allowed a businessman to stay open longer.

Standing on Main Street in Ramona, Oklahoma, the Masters Mercantile and Hotel provided lodgings upstairs and mercantile goods on the lower level. Like many business buildings in the late 19th and early 20th centuries, the Masters was a multipurpose establishment. Business owners learned to endure the ups and downs of the economy, which demanded they be flexible and creative. Sadly, today the building is no longer standing, and an empty lot is in its place.

The Rodecker Drug Company stood on one of Ramona's main street corners. With its catchy slogan, "If you need it we have it," Rodecker's was a mainstay of the community. The upper level contained offices and living spaces, as did many downtown business buildings in this time period. This structure succumbed to time and economic downturns in Ramona and no longer stands on the corner. Today the Caney Valley Museum occupies the spot. Some of the foundation slabs for the ornate corner columns still exist.

Located on the far eastern end of Eighth Street (now Don Tyler Avenue), the H.V. Myers building in Dewey was originally home to a lumber company. Then the building was used by the unionized employees of the Portland Cement Company. Pool tables and a bowling alley were added to the building. Later the building was home to the Dewey Public Library until its new structure was constructed on the west side of town. Today a floral and gift shop calls the building home.

Located on the corner of Eighth and Shawnee Streets in Dewey, this corner building in the Bartles block was home to Arcade Clothing. Below, the street-facing windows also advertise lumber, hardware, plumbing, tin shop, food, and furniture. This kind of general store was the forerunner of the modern mega-markets that sell all goods. The upper level contained offices and dwellings. Currently, Peter's Ace Hardware calls the building home.

With neoclassical elements and a tall spire upon its roof, the Security National Bank sits at the corner of Eighth Street (now Don Tyler Avenue) and Shawnee Street. Boasting a once-grand entrance with classical pillars and tall windows, the bank was independently operated until 1930, when it merged with the First National Bank of Dewey. Today the building's facade is encrusted in sheet metal, a hallmark of the 1960s and 1970s urban renewal programs. The building has housed a candy shop and is now home to a fabric shop.

This photograph of the first city hall in Bartlesville, Indian Territory, was taken on February 29, 1904. A single-story brick building, the city hall was located at 122 West Second Street. Later the city hall would move several times to accommodate the growth of the new town of Bartlesville, Oklahoma, once statehood was achieved. Today, like many historical structures, the building has been heavily remodeled and altered, and it is difficult for the untrained eye to recognize it.

The Carr/Bartles Mill, the first major business in what would become Bartlesville, was constructed in 1872 by Nelson Franklin Carr. Carr and his family immigrated to Kansas in 1859, and during the Civil War, Carr served in both the 6th Kansas Infantry and Cavalry units. An acquaintance of Jacob H. Bartles, a veteran of the 6th Kansas Cavalry, the two men would meet again in the Indian Territory. After establishing the mill, Carr sold his holdings to Bartles, and the genesis of Bartlesville's north settlement was born. Today all that is left are foundation stones along the river bank.

In 1884, Bartlesville early settlers William Johnstone and George B. Keeler built a single-story, wood-frame store. Located on the west side of North Delaware Avenue, the store was a dealer in dry goods, groceries, clothing, shoes, hats, farm implements, wagons, harnesses, hardware, glassware, crockery, and livestock. In 1895, Davis Sewing Machine was a tenant in the store. A replica of the store was constructed in Centennial Park to commemorate Bartlesville's Indian Territory days. Today the original location is a lot.

The Bartlesville Ice Cream Company was located on the northeast corner of Second and Osage Streets in Bartlesville. Owned by Lew Rittersbacher, the business provided Bartlesville residents with ice cream, which was a delicacy in the late 19th and early 20th centuries. Before the advent of iceboxes and refrigeration, ice cream was a special treat. The original structure passed from sight long ago, and today a small block structure housing an office stands in its place.

The Price Electra Welding Company was located at 118 Second Street in Bartlesville. Founded by H. C. Price, the company developed and perfected a method for the electric welding of pipe. During World War II, the company was the world's leader in the process and was one of the largest pipeline contractors. By 1956, the company had moved to its newly constructed headquarters at Price Tower. The original building stands today in the same location.

On the southwest corner of Third and Keeler Streets, the Landers Brothers Grocery and Palace Hotel served Bartlesville for generations. Over the years, several structures have stood on this location. Most recently, the Sunway Hotel Group has broken ground on a new multimillion-dollar hotel for downtown.

The Johnstone Building was built in 1910 on the corner of Third and Johnstone Streets, the same location of the Right Way Hotel. Here H. M. May founded Model Clothiers, a men's store. Later renamed May Brothers, it was Oklahoma's oldest family-run clothing store in operation in the same location. In 2008, the business closed, finishing a 99-year run in Bartlesville. Sadly, in August 2009, a fire swept through the building. The building is still owned by the May family, and all of Bartlesville has mourned its fate.

The Keeler Building, located on the northeast corner of Third and Keeler Streets, was purchased by George Keeler for $22,000 in 1906. Built in 1905, the Romanesque structure features exquisite brickwork. According to some historical accounts, it was in this building that the famed Statehood Day shoot-out took place on November 16, 1907, in which Ernest Lewis was shot and killed by deputy marshal Fred Keeler. Other historical accounts place the event across the street, next to the livery stable.

Open for business in the summer of 1904, the American National Bank sat on the northeast corner of Third and Johnstone Streets in Bartlesville. In 1909, a third story was added, and Union National Bank acquired American National. In 1920, the current structure was built. One notable tenant was Foster Oil, the company founded by oil magnate H. V. Foster, who would later build La Quinta. Currently Arvest owns the building, and in 2005–2006, the building was restored to much of its original condition.

In 1909, J. A. Vreeland purchased two lots on the northwest corner of Dewey and Third Streets for $50,000. Neither of the lots were improved, and previous owners, understanding that the value of land in the developing town of Bartlesville was at a premium, made immense profits on their sale. Vreeland then erected the Lannom Building on the corner, and the building became an anchor. Today nothing remains of the original structure, and the corner is now home to Ettinger's office supply.

The Owens Building was constructed in 1907 on the northeast corner of Third Street and Dewey Avenue. The Bartlesville State Bank was the most prominent tenant, with its entrance cut on a 45-degree angle. The upper floor was home to the Knights of Pythias, along with a chiropractor. Today the building still stands watch over a bustling community. Even after remodeling on the lower levels, the building's footprint is still recognizable.

Located in the 200 block of Third Street, the Kress Building was constructed by the Kress Syndicate of New York in 1912. The building was home to the company for more than 40 years. This two-story building features intricate, Louis Sullivan-inspired iron work that can still be seen. Another unique feature of this building is the interesting facades. With two distinct rooflines, the building gives the illusion of being two different buildings. Until recently, the building housed Bartlesville Office Supply.

Since 1919, the J. E. Curtis Building has stood on the northwest corner of Third and Osage Streets. The Curtis Supply Company specialized in selling automotive parts. By 1938, Bill Beasley began selling sporting goods as well. Sporting goods proved to be an enormous success, and the Curtis Sporting Goods store was born and was in operation until 2005. The building has undergone a recent renovation and now contains commercial space on the first floor, with loft apartments in the upper levels.

In 1903, the Vitrified Brick Company of Bartlesville was founded, and from this time forward, brick was the building material of choice in town. The Bradley and Bryant Building, constructed in 1903, is located on the corner of Dewey and Third Streets. The upper floor was known as the Bradley and Bryant Opera House and was the first theater in Bartlesville. The building was home to Mendell Hardware and the first spiritualist church. The building still stands, flanked by the recently renovated McAllister Block.

Located at 109 East Third Street, Betts Clothier was the first business to occupy this stately building. Storefronts were located on the street level, with offices and living quarters occupying the upper stories. Delokee Oil and Gas, Copan Oil and Gas Company, H. C. Moore Insurance Surety Bonds, Sweickley Oil Company, Starr Drug, and Koppels Style all called this location home. In 2000, the lower level was once again renovated and opened for business. Sweet P's gift shop is the current occupant.

Founded in 1905 by Herbert F. Tyler of Junction City, Kansas, the Portland Cement Company was located east of town near plentiful limestone, shale, and clay deposits. With land secured in 1906, the plant was constructed and became a major employer for Dewey and the surrounding communities. In February 1908, the Dewey Portland Cement Company produced the first concrete in Oklahoma. This plant featured the first use of concrete silos to store concrete in the world. Today the site is an oil field pipeline supply company.

The Masonic Building (Cities Service) was designed by Walton Everman. Built in 1918 at 401 Southeast Dewey Avenue and towering nine stories, the building's two top floors were a Masonic Lodge, which remain largely intact. The building housed oil businesses, including Empire Oil and Gas, Indian Territory Illuminated Oil Company, and Cities Services. It was renamed the REDA Pump Building when that company headquartered there. In 2004, Rogers State University purchased the structure. Today it houses the Bartlesville RSU campus and small businesses.

The second city hall building stood on the northwest corner of Fourth and Dewey Streets. With four domed corners, the building was home to city hall, the chamber of commerce, the fire department, the police department, and the jail. The fire department section boasted four large doors that opened toward Fourth Street to allow horses and wagons a running start. Sadly, the building was destroyed by fire in the late 1970s and now is a corner parking lot.

The Pioneer Building was constructed in 1910 on Dewey Avenue by the Pioneer Telephone Company. This three-story brick structure featured a sandstone veneer facade adorned by seven pilasters crowed by blue bells. The building housed the Pioneer Telephone Company until the 1960s, as well as a pharmacy. In the 1960s, much of the lower level original facade was removed. In 2004, the building was purchased, and a facade similar to the original was constructed.

Described by its architect as "the tree that escaped the crowded forest," the Price Tower was commissioned by H. C. Price, founder of the Price Company. Designed by Frank Lloyd Wright, the 19-story tower is Wright's only skyscraper. Price Tower was completed in 1956. Home to the Price Company and now to the Inn at Price Tower, Copper Bar, and the Price Tower Arts Center and Gallery, the building is on the National Register of Historic Places and is a World Heritage Site nominee.

CHAPTER 3

On the Move

Transportation

Built in 1899, this Santa Fe Railroad station is one of many found in small towns across America in the late 19th and early 20th centuries. For small towns like Copan, the railways and depots were the lifeblood of a community. Goods and passengers could be ferried about faster and more safely. Sadly, this depot is gone, as are the days of the steam locomotive.

Prior to the arrival of the railroad in small western towns, the horse and wagon or buggy were the main methods of travel. In every town, along with a good hotel, a restaurant, and a saloon, a livery stable was most important. Located in Ramona, the Blue Front Livery and Feed Barn served the needs of those traveling on horseback. Now the days of the livery stable have passed and so has the Blue Front.

Located at 122 West Second Street, the James Brothers Livery, Feed, and Stable was located close to Bartlesville's rail depot. The James family, pictured below, was comprised of, from left to right, a Mrs. James, Fannie James, Skimmie James, and W. M. James. In 1915, this two-story brick building was erected on the location and stands there today. Until recently, Red Dirt Soap Company called this location home.

With the development of the railroad into Indian Territory, towns like Copan, Dewey, Bartlesville, Ramona, and Ochelata were connected to neighboring states, and trade flourished. Every town in Washington County boasted a depot at one time. Below, the MK&T (Missouri, Kansas and Texas Railroad) depot in Dewey is shown. The view looks south. A grain elevator (right) is close to the tracks. Today the original grain elevator is gone, but a replacement elevator was built directly behind where the depot stood.

In 1909, construction on the Atchison, Topeka, and Santa Fe Rail depot began on Southwest Keeler Avenue in Bartlesville. The depot served Bartlesville as it grew with the oil industry. In 1946, the structure was covered in stucco by the Santa Fe Railroad. In 1971, the last passenger train passed through the depot. In 1983–1984, Phillips Petroleum Company renovated the structure and donated it to the Bartlesville Chamber of Commerce. Now it houses the chamber and the Bartlesville Convention and Visitors Bureau.

With the advent of the automobile, Phillips Petroleum began to cater to an ever-mobile public. Filling stations sprang up, and one of the most distinctive was the Phillips cottage-style station. This photograph shows the opening of the Phillips 66 No. 1 cottage-style station in Bartlesville in front of the Atchison, Topeka, and Santa Fe Rail depot. With 5 free gallons of gas and a line of waiting cars, the station was a great success. Now it is Frank Phillips Park.

With the birth of the oil and automotive industries, service stations became as iconic in American history as the automobile itself. Located on the corner of Third and Osage Streets, the Phillips Petroleum Station No. 4 served downtown customers. Featuring several large concrete pillars and an overhanging roof, the station bustled with activity. The Phillips 66 emblem was used on the building from 1930 to 1959. Today, due to recent renovation work, its concrete pillars were uncovered and remain partially exposed.

On the northeast corner of Fourth Street and Dewey Avenue, the Shell Service Station was a direct competitor to the Phillips Petroleum Stations. This view below shows the Pioneer Building in the background. The station is a time capsule, with its 15¢ gas and news of pilot Jimmy Doolittle on advertising boards. The station was eventually razed to make way for the Brilliant Bronze Filling Station in the late 1930s. Today the space is a parking lot.

Built in 1904 and boasting ornate brickwork, Baker's Automotive Dealership was the first of its kind in Bartlesville. Located at the busy intersection of Cherokee Avenue and Frank Phillips Boulevard, the building was most recently home to Oakley Buick-Pontiac-Jeep. Like many older structures, the facility was not able to meet the demands of the changing economy and automotive industry, and it now stands empty.

The Nellie V. Johnstone No. 1 Oil Well became the first commercial well in Oklahoma. On March 25, 1897, Jennie Cass dropped a go-devil into the well, and it came in a gusher. The Nellie V. Johnstone No. 1 produced more than 100,000 barrels. In 1947, it became a historical memorial. In 1948 and 1964, replicas were erected. For the Oklahoma Centennial Celebration, a fully functional cable tool-drilling rig was built, and Discovery 1 Park was born. A visitor center will be constructed in the park.

CHAPTER 4

A Place for All

Community Spaces

With the birth of towns like Copan, churches, governmental institutions, schools, and other places for community gathering developed. This early horse-drawn school bus from Copan shows the high esteem with which education was held by early citizens.

The Ramona Friends Baptist Church was built for $4,000 and was opened in 1905. On June 2, 1905, the church doors opened for worshippers, and they were treated to a new church with opera seats. Today the original wood-frame structure is no longer standing, and a new rock structure is in its place.

These two brick school buildings were constructed in 1904 in Ramona. The larger housed all grades and featured a cupola with the school's bell. The bell could be heard from a great distance. The smaller building contained a gymnasium, classrooms, and offices. By 1935, the cupola was missing on the large building, and it burned in a fire ignited by lightning. Today all that remains is the smaller building, which is now the administrative center for the Caney Valley Schools.

The Hotel de Hosley in Ramona, Oklahoma, was built in 1904 and originally contained 24 rooms. In 1905, when it opened, its owner eagerly began a new 24-room addition. The hotel was advertised as the most luxurious, well-appointed hotel on the Santa Fe rail line. After a third addition, its owner, R.W. de Hosley, boasted to the local papers that his hotel had a footprint larger than the entire town site of Ochelata. Today nothing remains of the grand hotel.

The Dewey Hotel's construction commenced in 1899 with the arrival of Jacob Bartles and his family to Dewey. They lived in a first floor apartment until the Bartles store and home were moved from Bartlesville's north settlement to the corner of Eighth and Dewey Streets. Jacob and his wife, Nannie Journeycake Bartles, were often seen on the hotel veranda. Completed in 1900, the hotel was operated for eight years, until Jacob Bartles succumbed to Bright's disease. Restored by the Washington County Historical Society as a museum, the hotel attracts visitors from the world over.

With neoclassical lines and design elements, the two-story Dewey High School was a feature of the community for decades. The school boasted two buildings and included a gymnasium as well. The land these structures were built upon was donated to the school system by Jacob Bartles after his arrival in Dewey. Today the buildings are no longer standing, and a modern children's playground for the Dewey Elementary School is now in its place.

The Paramount Theater was located on Eighth Street (now Don Tyler Avenue) in Dewey. Known also as the Yale and the Gem, the theater entertained generations. One could play bingo for 10¢ or 20¢ every Friday and take in a movie with titles like *Hitler: Beast of Berlin* and the Andy Hardy series. Today it is home to Barking Dog Design, an industry leader in museum exhibition panels and an active part of the downtown community.

Built in 1905, the Baptist church, located on the southwest corner of Fourth and Cherokee Streets in Bartlesville, boasted magnificent stained-glass windows. Dedicated in 1906, this was not the first church to grace this site. The original wood-framed structure was destroyed by fire on September 18, 1905. Through the years, the buildings erected on this site were torn down to make way for newer, larger facilities to minister to an ever-growing population. A church still calls this corner home.

In 1909, a four-story brick high school was built on Dewey Avenue between Tenth and Eleventh Streets. It featured towers with domed cupolas. From 1910 to 1926, the school prepared Bartlesville's youth. The last graduating class of 1926 included W. W. Keeler, the grandson of Nelson Carr (the first white settler in the area and the founder of the Carr/Bartles Mill) and George Keeler (the cofounder of the Keeler/Johnstone Store). The school was razed in 1939. Today the location holds an apartment complex.

Construction began in 1904 on a school for students in Bartlesville, Indian Territory. Completed in 1905, the Garfield School housed all grades. Bartlesville grew steadily, and by 1910, a high school was built. Garfield became an elementary school. A student at Garfield School for two years, young John Paul Getty sold newspapers and learned his hard work ethic that would make him a millionaire before turning 20. The school closed in June 1974 and was replaced by the Bartlesville Community Center.

Built in Italianate brick style, the three-story Bartlesville Civic Center/Library/City Hall was the center of civic and community life for more than 50 years. Erected in 1922, the civic center played host to traveling theatrical shows and stars, including the Ziegfeld Follies and Ethel Barrymore. It featured an organic-inspired copper awning reminiscent of the work of Chicago architect Louis Sullivan. By 1976, the auditorium was closed due to safety concerns. In 1992, a modern library facility was constructed in its place.

Bartlesville, like many other American communities, benefited from the generosity of steel magnate Andrew Carnegie. Formally opened to the pubic on March 13, 1913, the Carnegie Library was constructed on the southeast corner of Seventh and Cherokee Streets. After loving restoration, the law firm of Kane, Kane, Kane, and Roark calls this magnificent location home.

Opened on April 27, 1905, the three-story Almeda Hotel was located at the corner of Second and Johnstone Streets in Bartlesville. The lower level was home to the First National Bank. The hotel featured a French chef, elaborate dances on the weekends, and second- and third-story verandas. In 1930, the hotel contained 60 rooms that rented for $1 to $2 per day. The original structure has passed from the downtown landscape, and an automotive repair shop has taken its place.

Built in 1910 on the northeast corner of Dewey Avenue and Second Streets, the Buford Building was home to the Congress Hotel. A majestic three-story brick structure, the Congress was clean lined and simple, yet dignified. With 50 rooms in 1930, the hotel charged lodgers $1 to $1.25 per day. In 2009, the Buford Building saw new life as a restaurant. Frank and Lola's now occupies the street-level space and is part of a growing food and entertainment district in downtown.

Built in 1898 by William Johnstone and Ola Wilhite, the Right Way Hotel is believed to be the first Bartlesville hotel. Featuring 70 guest rooms, the hotel remained on the corner of Third and Johnstone Streets until the construction of the Johnstone Building at that same location. During its heyday, rooms could be rented for $1 per day. The Right Way Hotel was moved to the northeast corner of First and Osage Streets, and became a rooming house. In 2008, it was demolished.

The Maire brothers of Lima, Ohio, built Hotel Maire for $120,000. Opened in 1913 with 80 rooms, the five-story structure was popular with cattlemen and oilmen. By 1928, C. E. Burlingame had purchased it. Until 1973, it was operated as the Hotel Burlingame and charged from $1.50 to $4 for rooms. Under the Phillips Petroleum Company, the building became office spaces. The City of Bartlesville moved offices there in 2000. The Bartlesville Area History Museum calls the fifth floor home.

The Oklah Opera House, later known as the Liberty Vaudeville, was the brainchild of Jesse Overlees. Boasting a large stage, its grand opening in the fall of 1907 featured *Princess Pocohontas* for $5 per ticket. Ruby Darby, known as the "Queen of the Oilfields," performed frequently. Prior to the street's paving, ladies had a difficult time entering without dirtying their dresses, and men often watched as ladies lifted their skirts. Later the Oklah made the successful jump to motion pictures. Today the building has been replaced by green space.

Located at 304 Southeast Dewey Avenue, the Yale was one of many theaters in Bartlesville. Showing afternoon matinees, evening movies, and featuring titles such as the *Garden of Allah*, the Yale was built in 1915. Later in its career, the theater was called the Rex. The building next door was the KC Pool Hall. Both buildings have undergone numerous tenant changes over the years. Currently, the buildings house a resale clothing boutique and a jewelry store.

Located in the 500 block of Third Street (now Frank Phillips Boulevard), the Washington County Courthouse was built in 1909. Completed in 1913, the building was in use until 1973, when it was abandoned in favor of an updated structure. The building continued to be used by the U.S. National Guard, and in 1986, it was renovated and became office space. Now listed on the National Register of Historic Places, the Washington County Courthouse has stood proudly, watching over the citizens of Bartlesville for decades.

Built on land donated to the city by William Johnstone in 1906, a new baseball park was constructed in 1909. The original structure featured a wooden grandstand and fences. In 1932, a new concrete stadium was dedicated. Today Doenges Memorial Stadium plays host to various sporting functions, including national baseball tournaments.

CHAPTER 5

A MAN'S CASTLE

PRIVATE HOMES

This ranch home, located outside Bartlesville, was home to Nelson F. Carr and his family. Here Nelson Carr raised livestock, farmed, and planted various crops. While living on his ranch, Carr was concerned for the educational needs of children living outside of the cities and founded a log cabin school. In 1905, he and his family left their ranch and moved to Bartlesville. The house is no longer standing.

Founded by former 6th Kansas Cavalry trooper Jacob H. Bartles, the Bartles home and store was originally located in Bartlesville's north settlement along the Caney River. In 1899, after the course of the railroad was plotted, a disgruntled Bartles moved the structure to Dewey, a process that took six months. The Bartles home, store, and hotel were community cornerstones. Today the location houses the Tom Mix Museum, an Oklahoma Historical Society museum that attracts thousands of visitors annually.

Built at 311 South Creek, this two-story house with a wraparound porch was home to Nelson A. Carr. Along with his wife, Sarah, Carr came to Bartlesville and founded a gristmill along the Caney River. After selling his business to Jacob H. Bartles, Carr became a rancher, a farmer, and later an oilman. Carr bought the property from his son-in-law William Keeler in 1907. Now a metal-frame building stands on the location.

The Johnstone house has enjoyed an interesting life. William Johnstone was a true pioneer. Co-owner of the first mercantile south of the Caney River, Johnstone was a true entrepreneur. The home was originally built in 1887 on the 800 block of Cherokee Avenue. The house was moved to the 900 block of Cherokee Avenue to make way for Central Junior High School. Today the appearance of the house has been altered somewhat, but familiar elements still remain.

Frank Phillips came to Bartlesville from Iowa in 1903 and, after a series of initial setbacks, found success in the Oklahoma oil fields. The Phillips Petroleum Company became an industry leader. By 1908, Phillips began construction on a 26-room home for his family on South Cherokee Avenue. After the deaths of Frank and Jane Phillips, the home passed down to family who remained and preserved the home's history. In 1973, the building was donated to the Oklahoma Historical Society.

Built in 1925 of Indiana limestone, with many Georgian features, this home was a gift from Frank Phillips to his only son, John. This stately home features a columned archway entry that sets its facade apart from other homes in the neighborhood. A detached structure to the rear of the home is also in the same style.

John "Judge" Brennan was an attorney in Bartlesville who assisted in the acquisition of oil leases from the Osage Nation, which allowed the oil industry to prosper in Bartlesville. This home, located on Cherokee Avenue, was built for the Brennans in 1910. In 1922, the home was purchased by L. E. Phillips, the cofounder of Phillips Petroleum and brother of Frank Phillips. Under the ownership of the Phillips family, the home underwent renovations, and an oriental garden was installed to the rear of the home.

Early in Bartlesville's history, Cherokee Avenue was the location of many of the most stately homes. Built in 1927 for W. D. Reynolds, this Tudor-style home with a slate roof sits on the corner of Cherokee Avenue and Twelfth Street. Its most well-known owner was Armais Arutunoff. He was a Russian immigrant who founded the REDA Pump Company in Bartlesville. A noted inventor and philanthropist, Arutunoff and his family purchased the home in 1939. Today the home is exquisitely maintained.

Located on Hillcrest Avenue, this stately home features a central turret. It was built by C. E. Burlingame as a wedding gift to his daughter, Ruth Burlingame. With Tudor-stylistic influences, the home is unique amongst its neighbors.

Built in 1915 for the owner of the Burlingame Hotel, C. E. Burlingame, this three-story home features a third floor ballroom. This English garden–style home also features a tower with parapets. From 1940 to 1969, the home was owned by H. R. Straight. Straight was the president of Cities Service Oil Company, a major competitor of Phillips Petroleum.

Once the wealthiest man west of the Mississippi, H. V. Foster began construction on his grand home in 1930. La Quinta boasted 32 rooms and 14 bathrooms. Completed in 1932, the home was the center of Foster family life. His widow, Marie, lived there after Foster died in 1939. Now owned by the Wesleyan church and listed on the National Register of Historic Places, La Quinta forms the core of Oklahoma Wesleyan University as the campus administrative center and library.

This home in Ramona, built on 412 Second Street in 1909, was an Indian land allotment. Original owners George Sherrick, a barber, and his wife, Ruby, a first grade teacher, were the first to own an automobile in Ramona. Tommy and Mary Crabtree purchased the home in 1949 when Gene Crabtree, the present owner, was 10 years old. Most rooms have the original trim, baseboards, doorknobs, and some light fixtures. The flower medallions and brick that frame the home was from one of the original three Ramona banks. (Historical photograph courtesy Jo and Gene Crabtree.)

The two-story wood-framed structure (shown below) was once owned by the Beck family. It holds a unique distinction; the upper floor was used as a hospital, and the physician who traveled from Kansas to tend patients here was Dr. George Tann, of *Little House on the Prairie* fame. Dr. Tann was known to stay in this home while seeing patients, sometimes for several days at a time before returning to his family in Kansas. Sadly, the structure is now lost.

www.arcadiapublishing.com

Discover books about the town where you grew up, the cities where your friends and families live, the town where your parents met, or even that retirement spot you've been dreaming about. Our Web site provides history lovers with exclusive deals, advanced notification about new titles, e-mail alerts of author events, and much more.

MADE IN THE USA

Arcadia Publishing, the leading local history publisher in the United States, is committed to making history accessible and meaningful through publishing books that celebrate and preserve the heritage of America's people and places. Consistent with our mission to preserve history on a local level, this book was printed in South Carolina on American-made paper and manufactured entirely in the United States.

This book carries the accredited Forest Stewardship Council (FSC) label and is printed on 100 percent FSC-certified paper. Products carrying the FSC label are independently certified to assure consumers that they come from forests that are managed to meet the social, economic, and ecological needs of present and future generations.

FSC
Mixed Sources
Product group from well-managed forests and other controlled sources

Cert no. SW-COC-001530
www.fsc.org
© 1996 Forest Stewardship Council

Find *Your* Place in History.